Venust Heart

A Collection of Love Poems & Storytelling Verse

Shannon Sterling

BookLeaf Publishing

India | USA | UK

Made with ❤ on the BookLeaf Publishing Platform
www.bookleafpub.in
www.bookleafpub.com

Dedication

To my heart, spirit, and soul. To the brave ones who choose to heal, grow, and love in the face of pain. May we all discover the beauty of our existence and the light within us that can never be dimmed. This collection is for you—those who know the struggle but rise stronger with every step. And to the love that transcends all things: may we continue to find it in ourselves and in each other.

Preface

This collection of poems reflects my journey from darkness into light—a journey of transformation, self-love, and spiritual awakening. Each verse carries the weight of my experiences—my pain, my healing, my resilience—and the profound truth I discovered along the way: love, authenticity, and healing are not only possible but essential to our being.

These poems are for anyone who has ever felt lost, broken, or alone. May they serve as a reminder that within you is the power to rise, heal, and embrace your truest self. Through these words, I share my soul with you in the hope that you will find your own path to peace, love, and the beauty that lies within.

Acknowledgements

I am deeply grateful to all the souls who have crossed my path and helped me remember who I truly am. Thank you to my mentors, my spirit, and the universe for guiding me through the trials and triumphs that have shaped these poems. And finally, thank you to you, the reader, for taking this journey with me. May these words inspire you to embrace your own truth and walk forward with love, light, and resilience.

1. Love letter

Gentle soul, my angel in disguise,
Your soul carries a softness, beautiful and beyond what I
can inherit.

You're the perfect balance—a silent storm, a gentle spirit,
The ferocity within your balance holds the beauty of
your world.

You're the kind of beauty that rests at love's core,
Encompassing peace, soothing the soul evermore.

A divine rarity—I am grateful you exist.
Your soul is a beauty to behold.

2. Finding the words

Nothing compares to the sacred love I hold for you.
You are the stars, the moon, and the sun—all in one.

My soul is your soul, intertwined and whole,
And no words exist, in this world or the next,
To capture the way I love you.

3. Venust heart

You were in my dream again,
You were a forest by a moonlit beach.

I stood at the opening of the forest,
A breeze carried in by the crash of the ocean waves
behind me.

Inside the forest, the stars held the moon,
Radiating their quiet, eternal light.

Then I felt you—
Fiery chills coursed through my body.
I couldn't see you, but I could feel your venust heart.
I could feel your soul filling the spaces of my lungs.

Beneath my feet, roses began to grow,
Their vines wrapping around the tall forest trees.
You were everywhere and nowhere, all at once.

You were the melody of the forest,
A synchronized tune of my heartbeat.

4. Angel

The petals fell through her tears,
The feathers in her wings began to fall.

Her face sank heavily into her subtle hands,
For the first time, her light dimmed.

The grass reaching heavenward wilted beneath her,
With each tear it held.

Her heart was stunned,
Overcome with an overwhelming sadness.
For love had awakened her—
Deceived by true love's kiss.

5. Ethereal

You appeared to me like a dream,
It was truly love at first sight.

You felt so familiar,
As if we'd known each other before—
Perhaps in another lifetime.

I could question whether you're from this world,
Your ethereal soul,
Radiating like the sun itself.

The golden aura surrounding you—
How could I miss you?

Your beauty stuns me,
The kind of beauty that flows from within,
Painting your very existence.

Your ethereal soul—
How incandescent my heart becomes in your presence.

6. Abyss

A void of endless darkness,
Forever falling, never reaching the bottom.

I could scream, but no one would hear,
The abyss is where the forgotten go,
A place where souls go to die,
A cycle of pain that repeats.

Must I escape, or learn to embrace?

The abyss is a transcendental place,
A place to transform, to alchemize.
A loop of dark to light,
A cycle to break, a path to ascend.

Not a bottom to reach, but a peak to climb,
Only to become your highest self.

7. Transcendental

I was alive, but I couldn't breathe,
Clinging to the rope as lashes tore against my back.
"My strength won't slip," I whispered,
Tears falling with each strike.

I gave in. The light beside me dimmed.
I dropped to my knees, palms raw from my tears.
Their laughter sawed into my heart,
Their words like knives carving my soul.
My breath began to dissipate.

I surrendered, becoming transcendental.
The battle was within.

Slow and heavy, my breath returned.
My legs were weak, but I rose.
The glistening wind carried me into the dark,
Vowing to be the light that illuminates it.

8. You

Your mystery couldn't stop me from seeing beneath the
armored sun,
The distant skies, holding the stars as we both see.

Sunrises and the moon still share the sky,
Your existence paints the night in velvet.

It's as if your soul was crafted from divinity,
Perfectly woven into the fabric of love itself.

9. Beneath the arch

I was resting in my garden,
My back pressed against the rose-wrapped arch,
With the book resting gently on my lap.

The sun folding into hues of peach,
With soft grass beneath me—
How could I not rest my eyes?

Peace is so beautiful—
What is more tranquil than peace?
What could be more beautiful than the sun touching
water before it sets?
What could be more ethereal than a healing soul or a
love-filled heart beneath a rose-wrapped arch?

10. Beauty

You'll find my beauty within my soul,
Within my inner workings,
The very grace I hold.

In the twilight of my spirit,
In the boundless essence of my charisma,
And in the orphic trance of my aura.

11. Loves illusion

I looked beyond the veiled mask,
What I saw: that
Love doesn't hurt you.

Love only knows how to love.
It is healing, nurturing, kind—
The breath of life.

12. Bewitched

12

You have bewitched me,
I crave the very breath of you, incomprehensible though
it may be.
You are the light to my dark,
The moon to my night's sky.

The potion of love flows from your soul to mine—
You have bewitched me.

13. I love you

I cannot escape the way I love you,
No matter what direction I run,
My path will always lead back to you—
This deep desire for you.

You anchor my mind,
My every thought is of you.
You are in my bones,
Woven into the very existence of me.

You are like oxygen,
And if you must know anything,
Know this: I love you.

14. Universe

In my eyes, I could see the universe,
An ocean of ripples reflecting everything that I am,
Tides of change,
Shores of divinity.

In my eyes, I could see the universe—
The ripples of love,
Mounds of peace.

I saw my soul staring back at me,
I saw the world reflected through my eyes,
I saw my spirit holding itself.

I felt my emotions filling the spaces of my heart,
I saw the universe mirroring back at me—
The span of my existence, all through my eyes.

15. Distant lover

Every night, my feet grazed the sweet grass,
My eyes looked towards the stars,
Thinking of you.

Every night, my heart filled with grace,
Knowing that one day, our souls will finally meet—
My distant lover.

16. Darkness

I feared the darkness for what I could not see,
But seeing doesn't involve the eyes—
Seeing is an understanding.

Seeing is learning,
Seeing is a feeling.
So I looked into my darkness and discovered beacons of
light.

Born from pain and experiences I could not forget,
I heard the chains, like anchors, on my feet,
But then I looked closely and realized:
The darkness doesn't shackle,
It only wanted me to see that I was always free.

17. Cupids cloud

I sit in my garden, high above, on a heart-shaped cloud,
The sun pours through my chest—
No one can hurt me from this height.

Shielded from those who cannot love,
From those afraid to love,
From this cloud, I launch my arrow of love and healing.

Into the hearts of those who cannot love,
Into the hearts of those who fear to love,
And into the bruised, the broken hearts,
I open them with my Cupid's bow.

18. True love

All the times I searched for love, I never thought to look within.
I sought love in others,
Hoping to receive the same love I gave—
But it never returned.

My elixir of love ran dry,
And there was nothing left of me,
Just a sunken void, waiting to receive the love that never came.

I never realized the love I needed was already within me,
I only needed to love myself back.

19. Numb

For a while, my heart stopped beating.
I was alive, yet I felt nothing,
And numbness took its place.

All the flowers that once bloomed have wilted,
The array of lights that once surrounded my heart faded
to darkness,
Replacing warmth with a cold brush.

The harmonic beats stilled into silence,
What was once whole is now contorted—
A mosaic of wounds and scattered scars.

20. Kissing you

I could feel the softness of your heart unfolding through
the layers of our kiss—
I could taste the sun seeping through you,
I could taste the moon and stars on the waters of your
tongue,
As galaxies formed from the clash of our breath.